Will Young

Will Young

By Public Demand

Richard Galpin

CONTENDER
BOOKS

© 19 Merchandising Ltd 2002
Management: Simon Fuller at 19 Management Ltd

First published 2002 by Contender Books
48 Margaret Street
London W1W 8SE
www.contendergroup.com/books

This edition published 2002
1 3 5 7 9 10 8 6 4 2

ISBN 1 84357 032 7

Design by designsection, Frome, Somerset
Colour separations by Radstock Reproductions Limited, Midsomer Norton, Somerset
Printed and bound in Great Britain by Butler & Tanner Limited, Frome and London

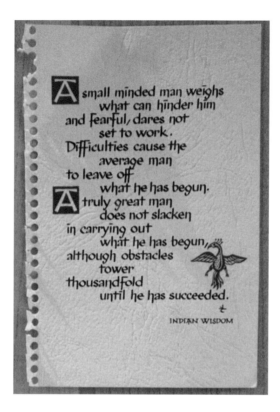

A small minded man weighs
what can hinder him
and fearful, dares not
set to work.
Difficulties cause the
average man
to leave off
what he has begun.
A truly great man
does not slacken
in carrying out
what he has begun,
although obstacles
tower
thousandfold
until he has succeeded.

INDIAN WISDOM

Acknowledgements

To all the people I work with on a regular basis – they are all great at their jobs and I know only too well if it wasn't for their hard work I wouldn't be doing all this, and if it wasn't for their great sense of humour, I would be in a madhouse! Actually...maybe I am! Richard, Faye, Charlotte, Olivia, Lucy, Jenny, Catri, Alison, Ned, Richie, Jacqui, Leighton, Jon, Lou, Cat, Julian, Charty, Helene, Ben, Margot, Daisy, David Venni, Simon Fuller, Nicki Chapman

Will

A big thank you to Anthony, Carlos, Charlotte, Faye, Jenny, Rebecca, and of course the very special Frances, without whom...

Richard

contents

chapter one

Stop stalling Richard and get on with the book –
time is money!!

Time: 12:07

<WILL>

It's 9am on a showery Wednesday morning, and my first meeting with Will in a café in Battersea, South London. The early start is because he has rehearsals all day for his performance at the Queen's Jubilee concert. It's not the most salubrious of eating venues, the walls decorated with signs that say 'Calories? Who's counting? This is a diet free restaurant!' and 'Our portions are enormous! Indigestion tablets available on request'. Hardly the sort of place you'd expect a singer who's released the fastest selling single of all time – 1,108,000 copies snapped up in its first week on sale – to frequent. Surely an upmarket Islington bistro would be more his scene, or a designer hotel where a cappuccino sets you back £6 – £7 if you want a sprinkling of chocolate.

"...the fastest selling single of all time – 1,108,000 copies snapped up in its first week on sale" [Evergreen/Anything Is Possible]

Will arrives 10 minutes early wearing a long green coat and grandad style flat cap. His entrance is clocked by three paint-splattered decorators who, with the subtlety of a 3am Girl, stare and nudge each other, their sausage-filled forks left hanging midway between plate and mouth. Will takes a table in the corner of the restaurant and sits with his ear glued to his mobile phone, presumably nodding to some imparted piece of information. Then again looks can be deceiving.

"I've become pretty good at pretending to talk to people on the phone," he laughs, his face splitting into that unmistakable banana grin, as we're introduced. "It's a trick I've learnt so that I appear busy because otherwise I can feel quite self conscious. At times I just sit there nodding at my phone."

Believe it or not, while the majority of the nation spent every Saturday at

"I've become pretty good at pretending to talk to people on the phone"

6.10pm glued to ITV to follow the soap-opera like goings-on of a bunch of singing hopefuls, there was a small section of the populace not fascinated by Darius, Gareth et al or the altitude of Simon Cowell's waistband. I have to confess I was one of them. Will Young? In my opinion, a grinning buffoon occupying far too many column inches in the newspapers. But of course opinions are like feet – everybody's got them and they can easily change direction. And after a while in his company you realise why everyone who has worked with Will or has met him thinks he's a thoroughly 'nice bloke'. He's open minded, but has a clear idea of where he is headed. In mid-sentence he can be both serious and light hearted and can say really funny things with such a straight face you're not sure if he's joking or not. He's good mannered, a clear throwback from his home counties, middle-class upbringing, and he's constantly questioning if he's being rude (for

example the phone rings while we are talking and after a brief chat he finishes by turning to me and saying "I'm so sorry that's terribly rude I shouldn't have taken that call"). And rather than just wanting to prattle on about his successes and how great he is, he's actually interested in what you've been doing. A refreshing change from the majority of egotistical music artistes who constantly need to be reminded how wonderful they are.

> "…you realise why everyone who has worked with Will or has met him thinks he's a thoroughly 'nice bloke'."

As breakfast is served (for the record the portions were by no means 'enormous', in fact Will questions the waitress whether there are two eggs in his small lump of scrambled eggs) Will fires off one anecdote after the next, most of them about his appearance the night before on a recording of the *Brian Conley Show*.

"On the first take I ran down the steps almost falling over, and as I was about to shake Brian's hand he just turned to me and went, 'You've got to do that again, this time slower'," he says making a point of covering his mouth with his hand as he chews on his toast. "When I sat down Brian produced a pint of Young's Bitter. I made a joke about the fact I prefer Brakespear and couldn't drink it. When I got backstage all that people were interested in was why I wouldn't drink the pint. It's got nothing to do with what make it is, or management not letting me drink, it was just that I'd never drink and perform. It's just something I wouldn't do." The world's fascination with Will's every move is unrelenting.

It's three days before he takes the stage with the cream of international singing talent at the Jubilee concert at Buckingham Palace and he's already a little nervous, as he hasn't yet learnt the words to *I Heard It On The Grapevine* and *We Are The Champions*, which he'll perform in front of a 12,000-strong patriotic audience and millions of TV viewers as well as people in the street. Although he's tickled that the succession of shows has been officially called

'A string of pearls' and he lets out a raucous laugh that again stops the decorators mid-bite. "I called a friend to tell her what they had called the concerts and she was like, 'That's a bit rude for a Royal do isn't it?!'"

The Jubilee performance is just the latest in a long, tiring schedule that has been laid out in front of Will from the moment he finished singing the last notes of *Light My Fire* and 4.6 million members of the general public decided that this boy from Hungerford was to be their 'Pop Idol'. There was barely time to celebrate his win before he hopped on a plane to Cuba to film the video for his first single *Evergreen/Anything Is Possible*.

Still one of the most memorable things for Will from those first few heady days of pop stardom in March 2002 is his first performance on *Top Of The Pops* – for any child nurturing a pop ambition, it still remains the ultimate goal. Even cool US rock bands who sniff in disdain at doing international TV commitments, admit that playing *Top Of The Pops* remains a high point in their career.

"I loved doing *Top Of The Pops*," says the 23-year-old. "It's what I've grown up with, it's such an institution. Although I do think there's room for another music

show on TV, I remember *TFI* was really good for bands, and so was *The Word*. The ultimate for me now would be to appear on Jools Holland. I remember he once played at one of the freshers' balls at Exeter university and all evening I was in the bar next door going, 'I love Jools Holland' and talking about his TV show, and then just as he was finishing his set, someone said 'He's next door, he's been there all night!'. But I didn't realise so I dashed next door to hear him going, 'Thank you very much and good night' before walking off stage." Perhaps Will is a little slow on the uptake.

Later that month, Will went out on the road as part of the *Pop Idol* tour – a 23-date, nationwide tour taking in Sheffield, Birmingham, Manchester, Glasgow, Newcastle and London. It was a chance for fans of the show to see the final 10 contestants – among them Jessica Garlick, Rosie Ribbons, Gareth Gates, Zoe Birkett, Darius Danesh – in the flesh. Each had solo turns before all teaming up on stage for a belting rendition of the Sinatra classic *My Way*. Tickets were like gold dust – 18,000 were snapped up for the first two Wembley gigs in just two-and-a-half hours.

"The tour was cool. We performed in the order you went out of the show, the first half was pop, the second big band. I really enjoyed it. People would come up to me and go in a sympathetic voice, 'How's it going? It must be tough', and it wasn't tough at all. I don't mind travelling, I'm used to driving long distances and I enjoy driving through the country with my Walkman on, staring out the window. Once you get over the first couple of nights, you get used to it and start to slip into a routine. It was great meeting up with everyone again, and the tour really cemented my friendship with people like Jess who I didn't know as well as Zoe and Hayley, and we got on so well. But I'm not going to talk about Jess anymore because every interview I've done I go on about how much I love Jess and it's getting boring now."

The whole gang travelled from show to show in one big tour bus and despite being in close proximity, there were no bust-ups or tearful tirade of insults, in fact everyone got on fine. Which is not very rock and roll.

"It was weird because people would get their positions on the bus the first day and generally stay there for the whole tour. The management sat up the front on the first table and then we'd be at the back. Teachers up front, naughty children at the back. The best drive was when we went from Manchester to Glasgow because I've always gone on holiday in Scotland. It was a beautiful day and it was weird because the last time I had made that same journey was two years ago, when I was halfway

through university, so it was cool to just reflect on how much has happened to me and how I could never have imagined where I would be today. It's good to have those moments when you sit back and reflect, taking the chance to remember how lucky you are."

Of course it wasn't all work, they still managed to find time to party after some of the shows, although Will is quick to point out that it wasn't wild drunken abandon every night. Just twice. And they were big time.

"Birmingham was a mess. Three old friends from uni came up and stayed, and we got wrecked. We ended up walking round the gardens at 4am. But we didn't have many parties. People probably think, 'Oh a tour means loads of parties'. We had one in Birmingham and an official one in Glasgow. My family came up to the Glasgow show and stayed at my hotel. We had a fire alarm in the middle of the night and the alarm was apparently ear piercing, but the only three people in the hotel who didn't wake up were me, my dad and my brother. The drunk Young men just didn't get up. The security guards were going to break down my door."

"…it was cool to just reflect on how much has happened to me and how I could never have imagined where I would be today. It's good to have those moments when you sit back and reflect, taking the chance to remember how lucky you are."

Will talks about the tour with a mischievous grin – he clearly enjoyed playing live with the friends he made on the TV show. Although he learned a valuable lesson about partying on tour. The morning after his drunken evening in Birmingham he had to get on board the warm tour bus and suffer a three-hour drive to Newcastle. There was only one place to find any sort of semblance of comfort.

"I'd been feeling a bit ill anyway and was massively hungover. I lay down in the kitchen at the back of the bus and slept because I felt so bad. I really was feeling rough. That night, I don't know how I managed to go on and perform at all. You know when you are hungover and your bearings go? Well at one point I couldn't work out where the end of the stage was. I came up on this platform and I suddenly saw the audience and just got the fear. I had to gingerly walk down the stairs and on to the stage. I think that evening was my finest performance – as I actually managed to get through the show without collapsing or being sick."

He admits it was the fans who got him through the more difficult shows – both evenings at London Docklands Arena he felt the atmosphere was a bit cold – particularly those who had lugged along enormous signs to hold up.

"The best one I saw was one that read, 'Get the shotgun Annabel' which was a famous quote about my parents I gave on the show, and the hilarious

"...I suddenly saw the audience and just got the fear. I had to gingerly walk down the stairs and on to the stage. I think that evening was my finest performance – as I actually managed to get through the show without collapsing or being sick."

"To see what an impact you can have on people's lives makes you realise what a fortunate position you're in – and it can impact on yourself as much as it can on the person who's met you."

thing was that my parents were sitting right in front of that banner," says Will. "We all got teddies and stuff like that thrown on stage, but we were warned not to pick them up as apparently there was an instance on a Spice Girls tour where one was thrown on stage which had a banger inside. But I always pick them up. I didn't pick up a pretty soiled pair of pants that some girl threw on the stage, which wasn't that pleasant. I'm not Tom Jones."

It was also a chance for less fortunate fans to meet the objects of their affection in person. Meet and greets are a regular part of a live tour where specially selected fans or competition winners pop backstage for a photo, a cuddle, an autograph and a few words with their hero. It was one such instance that made Will realise the enormity of the show

and how strongly it had effected some of the young people who were glued to their screens each week.

"At Wembley it was really difficult. There was a girl who came to see us who had been in a fire and had over a hundred operations. She was in a wheelchair and I was the last one to meet her. I couldn't really do it anymore, I started to get tearful. The nurse said, 'You don't know how much this means to her', and I could feel the tears coming, I'm awful at things like that. That was very emotional. To see what an impact you can have on people's lives makes you realise what a fortunate position you're in – and it can impact on yourself as much as it can on the person who's met you."

As he sips his orange juice, he suddenly becomes serious. It turns out

that the last night of the tour, at London's Docklands Arena, was a pivotal moment for Will. His non-stop, not-a-moment-to-catch-his-breath schedule had finally caught up with him. In an unbelievably short space of time he had gone from drama school student to the biggest name in pop music in the UK, which however strong a character you think you are is a lot to take in. And feeling worn out, and scarred by some comments made to his face and some which had been written about him in the press, he felt that enough was enough and he needed to stop and take stock of where he now was in his life.

"It all became too much. I hadn't had a break from the beginning of the show to the end of the tour. Various things happened along the way that made me quite self conscious at this time, and it was beginning to have an effect on me even when I wasn't working. It started off in a café in Kensington in the morning. I was sitting eating my lunch when this girl shoved her phone in my face and said, 'Talk to my mate!', and I said, very politely, 'I'm sorry, do you mind if I just finish eating my lunch'. Later on this guy came up with his phone and said, 'I'm so sorry, do you mind, but my girlfriend really loves the show, could you say hello to her?', and he was really polite so I did it. This other girl

> "It all became too much, ... it was beginning to have an effect on me even when I wasn't working."

then shouted across the café, 'Is it because I'm a girl?'. I turned round and said, 'No, it's because you are fucking rude'. The café went dead and stared at me. I just stood up and went, 'Well, I'll be leaving now', and made a gracious exit. Then, on the night of the show, I was coming up on the platform and I discovered somebody had written some nasty things about me on the wall. I then realised I needed time to sort out my head. I remember talking to my dad. I called him and asked what he was doing and he said, 'I'm in the greenhouse with a pint of Guinness having a lovely evening, I know it's boring old people stuff'. I said, 'Dad, you know what? That sounds lovely. I would give my right arm to be there'. I needed to go and sort things out in my head. There was a lot to take in – taking part in the show, winning the show, filming the video and then the tour. I just needed to take stock. Anyhow, I went to Italy with friends and had a brilliant time. It was just what I needed."

Will returned from his break with his head sorted out and ready to record the video for *Light My Fire*. In what would become a running theme in our chats, it's clear that Will is not another 'pop puppet' having his strings pulled. He's forthright about how he wants his career to progress and that means being involved in the selection process of who he works with. For this particular video, Will had no doubts that they'd chosen the right director.

"I was shown the director Bailey Walsh's showreel and I loved the videos he had done for Massive Attack and INXS, so I knew he was the right person. The video is very me in a lot of ways, he very cleverly got that. It's lots of strange people, having a party, shot in black and white, just having fun. The whole day was just a laugh. We had a sort of sports day and Bailey gave £20 each time someone won a race. I can still tell you which ones I won, I'm not competitive or anything, ha ha. I didn't win the first sack race but I won the next two. I won both wheelbarrow races and I would have won both piggyback races – the first one I did win but it was disputed and the second I let a little boy win. I won quite a lot of money but I used most of it to bribe the children who were racing with us not to beat me and then I left the last 40 quid in the DJ I was wearing. So somewhere a jacket is hanging up in a costume hire place with my money in the pocket."

With breakfast finished we exchange numbers and agree to meet later in the week. Will is off to a voice-coaching session on the other side of London and with heavy traffic it's going to mean a mad dash to make it on time.

"I've got an old push bike round the corner I'm going to get a lift on the back of that," he says completely deadpan. It takes a moment before you realise that he is actually joking.

chapter two

In Hampstead, just found a great pub – like being back in the country! Speak soon!

Time: 21:02

<.WILL>

"Somebody pinched my arse! What a cheek." Will is showing the exact place where an over-excited member of the *CD:UK* audience has tweaked a small part of his bottom. It's Saturday morning and he's in familiar surroundings. The London Television Studios is the place where Cilla introduces loud-mouthed and badly dressed lads and ladies in *Blind Date*, and where Angus Deayton attempts to keep order in *Have I Got News For You*. He's here to sing two songs – *Ain't No Sunshine* and *Light My Fire* – as well as record an interview with Cat Deeley. And while the backside squeezing may be a new experience, he's becoming an old hand at this sort of TV appearance.

"I feel comfortable in front of the camera. I think *Pop Idol* was a fantastic

"I feel comfortable in front of the camera. I think Pop Idol was a fantastic training ground"

training ground," he says. "All of the *Pop Idol* contestants have become like top SAS TV people – we go in, ask what the link is and do the job. I think we're really lucky that we got so much TV exposure early on."

Star 2 dressing room is at the end of one of the long, twisting and turning corridors that crisscross the upper levels of the studios situated on London's South Bank. If you don't have a map or a guide you'd get unfathomably lost. You can't help but think it was designed like this in the unlikely event that an intruder managed to sneak their way past security for a nose in Cilla's private shower or to see who was cavorting in Deayton's dressing room. They wouldn't stand a chance of finding it or finding their way out. In years to come you can imagine finding their skeleton slumped on the floor of a dusty, unused part of the corridor. The dressing room looks like it was modelled on a motorway travel tavern. There's a mini bar, sofa, bathroom and a wilting bunch of flowers – you wouldn't be surprised to find Alan Partridge sitting in the corner listening to Abba and clutching his 12-inch plate. On the wall are two modern paintings, where an artist has smeared a bit of red on a canvas and claimed it's his interpretation of 'sunlight over the Sahara'. To anybody else it's just a red smudge. But this is one of the better rooms, "It's not a poxy little one like we were in last time," laughs Will – that treat has been reserved for Westlife who are squeezed into the room next door.

Despite it being one of the bigger rooms, it's still full of people: there's Will's PA Faye Anthony, his make-up artist Helene Dean, record company TV publicist Ritchie Crossley and his stylist Charty Durrant. The team are used to working together and have been with Will on all his TV appearances to promote the two singles. They've nicknamed themselves the 'Clumsy Crew' as their time together is usually punctuated with comedy falls, broken glasses, large spillages and valuable items left behind on shoots.

"Honestly, you stick around for a while with us and I swear you will catch our disease," says Will. "Although today hasn't been too bad, two hours gone, and nothing broken."

Will is trying on outfits Charty has brought along for him to wear on the show, among them there's a Paul Smith suit jacket, an Ozwald Boateng jacket

and a cream and red Energie leather jacket. Will decides to ditch his scruffy jeans which have more holes than denim – "I think these are only to be worn on the farm now" – in favour of a brown John Smedley jumper and gray pin-striped trousers. Although he also takes a shine to a green, red and blue striped Paul Smith scarf, It's a sample from the winter collection and needs to be returned to the PR. The way that Will has his eye on it though and the way he keeps wrapping and unwrapping it around his neck, it's unlikely that this particular fashion item will find its way back to the fashion house.

"We change his styling depending on what he's doing," says Charty. "This morning he's dressed more loose and casual because that's the style of the

show and it will suit his performance. If we were doing something more formal I'd suggest we put Will in a tight suit jacket – probably a few sizes too small – so that he'd be stiffer and more upright."

This morning's show has more spice to it with the fact that Ant and Dec have returned to the programme that made them famous, to promote their England football anthem *We're On The Ball* and are this week vying for the number one slot with Will. Ant sticks his head round the door to say hello and the pair agree to meet up for a drink after the show.

The mutual respect is clearly evident.

"I think we're good friends," says Will. "They made me realise they weren't just being friendly to me because of the show or that it was just a job, as they've been really nice about me in interviews afterwards. I think they're good at their jobs and so professional, which I like. I like professional people. It's funny that we've both got singles out at the same time. I was going to go round and set light to their bins and leave a note saying, 'I've lit your fire', ha ha."

Despite a star-packed show (Will's

vocal warm-up is interrupted by the phone ringing, and someone asking to speak to Jenny Frost from Atomic Kitten), he's disappointed that Shakira is not going to be here singing *Whenever, Wherever*. He's recently become a bit of a fan of the Colombian diva.

"I saw her at *Top Of The Pops* and I thought she was fantastic. I wanted to go into her dressing room and say hello but didn't have the courage to do it. I was going to knock on the door and pretend to work for *TOTP* checking that everything was alright with her room, ha ha. In the end I stood in the corridor pretending that I was locked out of my room and fiddled with the door knob as she walked past. She's so tiny, like a little doll. I love her song especially the bit about her breasts being small and humble."

The call comes for Will to make his way down to the studio floor. On the stairs he bumps into Sophie Ellis Bextor, dressed in a Japanese silk kimono who's here performing her single *Get Over You*.

They give each other a friendly hello and she thanks him for the note he sent her. Sophie's make-up artist was part of the team with Will in Cuba where he recorded the videos for *Evergreen* and *Anything Is Possible*, and Will passed on a small card to Sophie saying hello.

Despite it being early on a Saturday morning, Will's voice resonates with clarity – there's no denying that this boy can sing.

In the frenetic mêlée of the studio, bottom squeezing teenage girls scream enthusiastically as Will is introduced. Today he's backed by a four-piece band who do all of his live gigs – Joseph, John, Thomas and Chris. Despite it being early on a Saturday morning, Will's voice resonates with clarity – there's no denying that this boy can sing. He seems to be able to pull the big notes out of the bag when you or I would be desperately taking a lungful of air. After a faultless performance and when the cheers have subsided he makes a point of thanking each member of the band and shaking their hand before a mad dash back upstairs to the dressing room.

The 'Clumsy Crew' are in a buoyant mood. It was a good performance – in fact, it's regarded as his best TV performance so far. Slick, polished and professional. Will is just as pleased that for the first time he has done a gig without dark sweat marks staining the underarms of his jumper. Like the winning captain at a cup final, he holds up his armpits for everyone to examine.

"Get a good look, it's the first time there's been no marking," he says. "Apparently there's an operation you can have done where they laser the sweat glands. I can't think of anything worse. Where would all the sweat go? It would just be running around inside your body."

The nip on his derriere was certainly a first for Will. Although it should be pointed out, it's not a life-threatening injury! "That's the first time that has happened. I get grabbed on the arm a lot though. I remember during the Gareth vs Will campaign I'd got off the bus when a girl grabbed my arm and wouldn't let go. I didn't want to just pull it away so I was like, 'Excuse me but you're really hurting my arm' and thankfully she let go."

After a faultless performance and when the cheers have subsided he makes a point of thanking each member of the band and shaking their hand before a mad dash back upstairs to the dressing room.

This morning's headline in *The Sun* newspaper reads 'Will aims to party just like Beckham'. It's a story about how Will reckons he's music's answer to David Beckham and that he plans to lift the nation just like the England skipper when he performs at the Jubilee. It's a headline that Will is

pleased with, as he admits, along with the rest of the nation, to having a bit of a fascination with Posh Spice's other half.

"He's a very good footballer and a very good looking man. It's become a joke amongst my friends. I was told that during *Pop Idol* both David and Victoria voted for me, so the joke grew out of that. I think they're both fantastic, they've produced a whole generation of people who look just like them – they've got the haircuts, the glasses and the clothes. It's weird. Anyway, my thing is that I would love to go to supper with them and when Posh is making crème brûlée in the kitchen I would hang out with David, ha ha."

Unlike David Beckham and his omnipresent wife, aside from the TV promotion and magazine interviews, Will is keen to stay out of the limelight. We discuss celebrity parties, and unlike the majority of famous faces around, Will doesn't want to face the wall of flashbulbs and have microphones shoved in his face at film premieres or restaurant openings. It's a game he just doesn't want to play. His only real

Will is keen to stay out of the limelight. We discuss celebrity parties, and unlike the majority of famous faces around, Will doesn't want to face the wall of flashbulbs and have microphones shoved in his face at film premieres or restaurant openings. It's a game he just doesn't want to play.

experience of it was at a party in Savile Row for one of his favourite designers, Ozwald Boateng.

"He very kindly asked me along and I really like his suits so I went. But I'm not sure it's really my thing. Some people there were really strange. At one point Ken Livingstone's PA came up to me and said, 'Ken would really like to have his photo taken with you,' and I went, 'Well only if Ken can explain how he intends to implement his five pounds a day charge to use London's roads because I don't think it's going to work'. I couldn't believe how cross she was. Later on I was approached by some showbiz journalists. I didn't know who they were before I was in *Pop Idol*.

They came up to me and started asking me questions and I was like, 'I'm sorry, I'm not working tonight, lovely to see you here but can I talk to you another time?'. The next day they had written this nasty thing about the fact that I won't be around in six months. So it makes you wonder what the point is in going to these things? The other thing that happens is people come up to you and just quote their job title and shake your hand. Maybe it's something you get used to in time – but why should it be? Journalists knock celebrities for turning up at everything and knock them if they don't. I'd love to sit down with them and find out what they really think outside of work. That's why I don't go to those things. I was asked to go to the Spider-man premiere and I want to see the film and will pay to go and see it. But I think they're meat markets and you just get hassled."

Will returns to the studio floor to film an interview with Cat. He's taking calls from the viewers and despite the fact that the show is aimed at teenagers, one of the callers is a 50-year-old fan who wants to know whether Will minds having older fans following his every move. He's gracious and polite in his answers, even when asked if he has a favourite joke, which clearly he hasn't, he seems unflappable as he turns and asks the audience if they have any winning gags. Later Will explains how enjoyable he is finding this sort of TV show.

"I don't normally try and think of things to say, I try and do it unplanned. Sometimes you will be told what questions you will be asked, like today I knew that caller number three was asking for a joke. Just before I went on I said to Cat that I didn't know any jokes so I was trying to drag out the first two callers hoping we wouldn't have time for the last call. Cat had an evil glint in her eye when she went 'And

"I really enjoy doing these sorts of interviews, I guess I just like talking to people."

now caller number three'. I really enjoy doing these sorts of interviews though, I guess I just like talking to people."

With the show over, Will is keen to leave the motel-like dressing room and catch up with Ant and Dec in the bar. The phone in the dressing room rings again. Will rushes over to grab it and puts on his best cock-er-nee accent.

"Hello, post office. No mate you've come through to the wrong room this is the post office. There's no Jenny Frost here."

If the music doesn't work, there will always be someone to step into Dick Van Dyke's shoes in *Mary Poppins*.

chapter three

SHIT, SHIT, SHIT, SHIT, SHIT!
(Feeling pretty confident!)

Time: 12:36

<WILL>

It's 3pm on Monday, June 3rd. The day of the Jubilee concert. A car has arrived at Will's West London home to take him to Buckingham Palace. The driver rings the doorbell of his flat and a slightly flustered Will answers.

"Look, can you just give me five minutes," he says before disappearing back upstairs. He's smoking. A lot. He pulls his diary from his bag and writes the words, 'Remember how far you've come'. Today is not just another performance in front of a few hundred people. Will knows it's more than that.

"I get very reflective with things like this. That's how I psyche myself up," he says. "I try not to get worried about mucking it up, it's just exciting and I want to soak the whole thing up. You know when it's somebody's wedding or

Today is not just another performance in front of a few hundred people. Will knows it's more than that.

Christmas is coming and you feel unlike at any other time of the year because you're so excited the whole time? Well this is how I've been feeling since the rehearsals last week. It's not often you get to play at Buckingham Palace – for the Queen."

A few deep breaths and a more settled Will gets into the car and makes the short journey to the palace. The entrance to the backstage area is through the Royal Mews (basically a posh name for the stables where the golden stage coach is housed). Understandably security is tight and all bags have to go through a large X-ray machine. A month prior today every person in each of the performer's retinue had a complete background search. If there's some best-forgotten conviction lurking in your background you won't be allowed in. Maybe that's why Mark Morrison is not on today's list of entertainers. The streets are already full of people waving flags, bedecked in Union Jack T-shirts. But Will seems distracted when asked for an autograph, his thoughts are on other things. Nerves are clearly getting to him. Once past the machines and security checks, he clambers on board a bright green people carrier for the drive through the gardens to where all the artistes have their dressing rooms. It's a strange drive as the cars are only allowed to travel in this part of the palace grounds at 5mph.

"This reminds me of *Jurassic Park*, where the electric trucks go through the park and are attacked by the T-Rex. Except all I think we might see here are a few aggressive Corgis," says Will as we trundle through the grounds at little more than walking pace. In fact it would be quicker to get out and actually walk. The cars drop us off at a covered walkway, which leads to the back of the stage and the cluster of marquees. Set back 100 yards from the others is the food tent, which is where everybody appears to be gathering. Will's on stage at 8.25pm for his solo performance but will return shortly afterwards to sing *We Are The Champions* with the surviving members of Queen.

"Phil Collins was originally supposed to sing the Queen song," says Will having a sip of herbal tea. "But he felt he had too much to do, he is going to be on stage for such a long time – nearly three and a half hours of drumming. So Phil suggested I sing it. When I heard that

I was really flattered. I remember thinking, 'If he thinks I can do it, then maybe I can.'"

The rehearsal two days prior was exhilarating for Will as much as it was nerve wracking. He joined some of the biggest names in British music over the past 25 years to prepare for today's gala. You get the feeling that at first he felt a little out of place, that unlike the other big names on the bill, he hadn't earned the right to be there. It's typical of Will's humility. But the respect that they showed him made him feel at home amongst such esteemed musical colleagues.

"We all went to this church in London, where the rehearsals were taking place and it was amazing. That was when I started getting over excited. Annie Lennox, Tom Jones and George Martin were there. The first time I had to sing *We Are The Champions* was in front of Roger Taylor. I was really nervous. The cast of the Queen musical *We Will Rock You* who were going to sing on this particular song were also there, and I couldn't help but imagine they were probably thinking, 'Who does he think he is?'. I was cacking it. But it didn't go too badly, there was one point where Phil Collins just gave me the thumbs up from behind the drums which made me feel great."

Sitting close by to Will is ageing rocker Eric Clapton eating a sandwich, while Tom Jones and Shirley Bassey

"I was cacking it. But it didn't go too badly, there was one point where Phil Collins just gave me the thumbs up from behind the drums which made me feel great."

sit nearby chatting and laughing. There have been some reports in the newspapers that today's concert is not indicative of British music, with a number of big names notable by their absence. But Will feels privileged to be part of such a landmark concert.

"I have so much respect for people like Eric Clapton who can walk up with just a guitar and do his thing. It's pretty amazing. I spoke to Annie Lennox about how when you are a performer you have to keep proving it. People must always be thinking, 'Hmm, I wonder if Annie or Tony Bennet have still got it', especially when you get older. But she does it every time and that's what I realise I am going to have to do. Keep proving myself."

He's also aware that, in going out on stage and taking lead vocals with Queen, he is, in effect, taking legendary front man Freddie Mercury's place. It's a role that could set him up for criticism from both die-hard Queen fans and the press who will attempt to compare him to the moustachioed and flamboyant singer.

"People can criticise my clothes and style and the sort of music I play, but if you sing well then that's the way that you prove you're any good. They can't say, 'You're crap at singing' because I can turn around and say, 'Well I'm not'. So I'd better sing well or else I'm screwed!"

Will retires to his dressing room – sparsely furnished with a leather sofa, clothes rail and mirror – to listen to the songs he's singing today on his portable CD player and to do some vocal warm-ups. It's notable that he doesn't eat. He admits he can't face food before performing, but the herbal tea flows. Once the show has finished, Will is taking a break. He's heading off to the South Of France for a week with his family. He's been feeling similar to how he felt at the end of the *Pop Idol* tour. It's been non-stop for three months and he needs another break to clear his head and again focus on where he's going. You get the feeling that these sojourns are vitally important to him. He's someone who is committed to making a success of his singing career, but there's only so much he can do before all the attention he receives starts to get on top of him.

"Last week I went out for supper with old family friends and their parents. They wanted to know what I'd been up to and I suddenly had a big stress. I realised that I was getting really fed up with 'me'. I felt if I had to do another interview all centered about me I would go insane."

His vocal preparation and thoughts of his impending holiday are halted by the need to do an interview for that bastion of children's TV, *Blue Peter*, who are here doing a number of face-to-face interviews back stage. The naughty glint returns to Will's eye and just as he sits down to talk to presenter Konnie Huq, he turns and whispers "I'm going to have some fun with this."

Will: "Right. I would like to say that I entered a sunflower competition when I was nine and my sunflower should have won because it was three feet higher than the one which did win. I would like to make an official complaint. I still have the photos to prove it."

Konnie (slightly taken aback): "Well we have the competition again this year."

Will: "Well I'm going to enter my sunflower and it's going to win. Because it's very tall."

Somehow you can't help but think he might just do that.

Buckingham Palace has served as the Royal residence since 1837 and in its 160-year history it has endured a hail of bombs from the German Luftwaffe, an errant para-glider landing in the gardens and a 32-year-old intruder contemplating suicide in the Queen's bedroom, but you could say that none of these compare to a poodle-haired Brian May standing on its roof blasting out a version of

"People can criticise my clothes and style and the sort of music I play, but if you sing well then that's the way that you prove you're any good. They can't say, 'You're crap at singing' because I can turn around and say, 'Well I'm not'. So I'd better sing well or else I'm screwed!"

"Now that I've done such a big show, I really want to do a little intimate gig. I felt a real connection with the audience and it kind of gave me confidence to go out and make them proud."

God Save The Queen on his guitar to kick start the Jubilee concert. It's like anybody else's birthday party except instead of a Karaoke machine and a selection of eighties' greatest hits, it's Brian Wilson, Rod Stewart and Paul McCartney holding the microphone.

By 7.30pm Will is waiting at the side of the main stage. He's on after Atomic Kitten and will be followed by Blue. As he waits in the wings, some of the audience in the front row can see who's next on and start to wave in his direction. Then one of the biggest cheers of the day rebounds off the Palace's walls as Will launches into *I Heard It On The Grapevine*, looking immaculate in a black suit with purple jumper underneath.

"Wow, that was pretty cool. It was nice to see everyone's faces and I was so pleased I got a nice reception," says Will, catching his breath before returning to the stage for the Queen song, which thankfully goes off without a hitch.

"As I was standing there I thought something that probably no one else performing here today did, that these people out here have actually put me here on this stage. Now that I've done such a big show, I really want to do a little intimate gig. I felt a real connection with the audience and it kind of gave me confidence to go out and make them proud. I've done the big gigs now, they're amazing things, but I want to do something smaller which shows people I'm the same

person. So it's not all about the glitz, it's about the music."

With his singing commitments finished, Will now takes time to eat – unfortunately, this singing business is clearly hungry work as there's precious little left. Will scrapes together a bit of chicken stew and some rice before heading to the special cordoned-off area at the side of the main stage to watch some of the acts. The trouble is, to reach the seats he has to cross the small stage at the side. The crowd immediately thinks Will is about to sing another song and goes mental. It takes some calming hand gestures from Will to quieten them down.

"This is brilliant," shouts Will, who's clapping along with Jo O'Meara from S Club 7 and Emma Bunton to Rod Stewart's *Handbags And Gladrags*. Will has struck up quite a friendship with the ex-Spice Girl after meeting her in rehearsals for the Jubilee show. "We've really bonded over this week," he says. "We were the only two solo artistes in the first half of the show and we have the same management company. She's the loveliest girl, so sweet."

Emma is equally complimentary about Will. It's like some big pop star love-in.

"Will is a really lovely guy. He's just really down to earth, I was glad he was there at the rehearsals as it gave me someone to talk to. His voice is incredible – it's a classic soul voice," she says.

As the big finale draws close Will grabs Emma's hand and pulls her on to the stage. They've been told to wander along to the far end, but instead just stay where they are and grab a microphone to join in the finale

"Will is a really lovely guy. He's just really down to earth ... his voice is incredible – it's a classic soul voice." [Emma Bunton]

...one of the biggest cheers of the day rebounds off the Palace's walls as Will launches into *I Heard It On The Grapevine*.

– a singalong to The Beatles' *All You Need Is Love* and *Hey Jude*. Later Will tells me that in his short music career, this was by far the highlight. The evening turns even more surreal when they are joined on stage by the Queen and her family who share a few words with each of the artistes.

"The Queen said something to me but all I caught was '...on TV' so I think she said, 'I've seen you on TV'. I couldn't really ask her to repeat what she'd said, ha ha," Will says when he comes off. "Charles was really nice, just like any friend's father, and Prince William was a normal 19 year old. We chatted for a bit, I guess we have a few things in common – he went to public school and I did too. He was like somebody I would have met at university. I didn't really get a chance to talk to Harry, but he seemed to be having a laugh."

It was a momentous night for Will. Singing *We Are The Champions* leaning on the shoulder of Brian May, backed by Ray Cooper, Phil Collins and Roger Taylor, was make or break time. "I really hadn't had much rehearsal time. It was just one of those occasions I had to rise to". He has much to reflect on during his week away.

chapter four

Ah the sun! The sea! The wine!

Time: 14:22

<WILL>

A short story about Will and his haunted holiday house: "I was staying in a converted monastery in the mountains just outside Cannes in the South of France. It was the middle of the night. I was fast asleep when I suddenly woke up to find the blood rushing in my ears, it was like someone was saying 'why, why, why' really quickly. It also sounded like someone was stamping on the floor. My heart was beating really fast. It is weird to describe, but it was like somebody had gone past me really quickly and made my heart jump up into my mouth and back down again. I'd heard this from other people, that this is what ghosts do, they sort of bring up your energy. I was shitting myself, I have a really bad imagination at the best of times, it runs away with me. I looked out my window, which had the curtains drawn, and in the moonlight I saw the shape of a cat run really quickly past the window. It was kind of like the ghost had gone, and I suddenly felt fine again. I think a ghost must have been just checking me out. I sat up in bed and said, 'If there are any bad spirits here in the room would you please leave'. That's what I heard you are meant to do. The strange thing is that the exact same thing happened to my brother who was sleeping in the next room. Now that's spooky. After that nothing much happened for the rest of the week, except the lights flickered now and then and I'm sure I could hear someone singing 'Evergreen, Evergreen' faintly in remote parts of the house. I found myself thinking 'is that young lad from Dradford playing a trick on me?'"

chapter five

Salut. Am back from holiday, feeling relaxed and raring 2 go! Just seen 7 ducks in a v – surely that is a good sign.

Time: 10:33

<WILL>

There are 100,000 fans wandering around Dublin city centre and they're in a fervent mood. The teenage girls wave brightly coloured banners, their faces painted with their favourite idol's name. The mood is jubilant, but for once they're not here for Will. At Phoenix Park the Irish are welcoming home the Republic Of Ireland football team from their World Cup adventure. Local boys Westlife, dressed in matching tri-colour suits, are on a hastily erected stage to belt out a patriotic rendition of *World Of Our Own* while team manager Mick McCarthy is presented with a Waterford Crystal vase for his team's stirling efforts.

In the Octagon Bar of the 140-year-old, recently refurbished Clarence Hotel (affectionately known as Bono's Place by the local taxi drivers, for the front man of the world-renowned U2 rockers is actually the owner) Will is nursing a pint of Guinness oblivious to the hoo-ha outside. He's not a big football fan. He's looking tanned and relaxed after his week away despite the unexpected supernatural experiences. The break has clearly done him the world of good; refreshed the batteries. A chance, for a few days at least, to revert back to annonymity, the French not yet having caught the *Pop Idol* bug. He's been here for two days, co-writing and recording tracks for his album which will be released in time for the Christmas rush. He likes Dublin, particularly the Irish's casual attitude to life. "It's definitely less manic here than in London and their mentality seems to be different."

Despite his casual demeanour, Will knows that this is a crunch time for him. It's when he should be fulfilling all of the potential the country and judges of *Pop Idol* saw in him by actually going into a studio to record his own material. There's no safety net of covering other people's already famous songs. These are Will's songs. And they are expected to be good.

"It's exciting to be writing for the album – going to the studio is nerve wracking as it's make or break time – but I'm enjoying ever minute of it. I've been over here writing once before, a few days after I got back from Cuba. On the first day we had written a song in just three hours and it was wicked. But I don't see myself as a writer as yet. All I can say is that the songs at this stage are turning out really great."

Behind an unremarkable door, 10 minutes from the centre of the city, is the home and studio of Richard 'Biff' Stannard. In 1992 he wrote and

"This is a crunch time for him. It's when he should be fulfilling all of the potential the country and judges of *Pop Idol* saw in him by actually going into a studio to record his own material. These are Will's songs. And they are expected to be good."

produced East 17's first two albums – including the singles *House of Love* and *Deep* which made their name – before teaming up with Matt Rowe for the Spice Girls' albums *Spice* and *Spiceworld*. He now writes and produces and remixes with Julian Gallagher, and they were two of the masterminds behind Kylie's single *In Your Eyes* and together did Emma Bunton's *What Took You So Long?* Five years ago they came to do some work here in Dublin and loved it so much that they decided to stay. Their home-cum-studio is designed to be laid-back and comfortable to encourage the creative thought process that goes on in between these walls. There's a big blue sofa jostling for position next to a piano, vintage, framed Flintstones cartoons are placed next to a Spice Girls platinum disc on the walls and, bizarrely, in one corner there's a life-size skeleton with a beaded hairdo. One of the rooms is dominated by a huge TV which is continually tuned to *Big Brother Live*, which Biff and Will have become addicted to. In between making music they discuss who should bc up for eviction, their bewilderment of Jade and, more importantly, who they couldn't stand to be stuck in the house with.

Will chooses Richard and Judy, Ant and Dec ("cos they're funnier than me") and Rory Bremner ("he'd continually be doing impressions"), and he's convinced that there would be some pretty ugly scenes if this happy group were living on top of each other. "I think I would end up killing somebody in there. I really would commit murder."

Biff and Julian are producers who can pick and choose which artists they work with. Recent visitors to their studio have been Bono, David Gray and The Corrs, and Biff admits that at first he was sceptical about working with somebody who had appeared on *Pop Idol*.

"We wouldn't normally work with someone like Will, but we just heard that voice and said, 'Yeah, why not?'. As a singer Will is way up there. There are very few young artists who, when we record with them, can sing through the whole song. You tend to do the verse, then the chorus and piece the whole thing together. But he sings it all. The only other artists we work with who do that are Gabrielle and Bono."

Will didn't really know of Biff and Julian's work before coming to Ireland but he shares their mutual respect, and feels it's down to good management that he's been put in touch with such great writers – he's also recording with Cathy Dennis (Kylie's *Can't Get You Out of My Head*) and Mike Peden (once of The Chimes).

"I was worried that I didn't know any of these people. The record company and management could have suggested anybody and I wouldn't have known what they were like. But so far it's been fantastic. I put my faith in people who know the industry. I've taken a lot of advice from my manager Simon Fuller. We're quite similar people in a way because we have very similar ideas. When we had our first meeting I turned up with a whole bunch of ideas and more than half of the things I had written down were what he was saying to me. It was so comforting that we were on the same wavelength, we work together. The press say we're told what to do but I don't know where that's come from. You get advice from the best people and you take it. It's just like any other job."

Will describes writing with Biff and Julian as an 'organic' process. The two producers will have the idea for a riff or a chorus, and then as a group they'll play around with the song and add

some lyrics that seem to work with the way the tune is progressing.

"I didn't have a clue about songwriting. I always thought I'd be able to write but I didn't know how to go about it. I can play the piano a bit but not enough to do a whole melody. But Biff and Julian will have an idea for a bridge and a chorus and we'll just jam, and that's the way I prefer to work, because I work really well with live instruments."

The results of the next few days will give a strong indication of exactly what Will Young's sound is going to be. Pop like S Club? Power ballads like Meat

Loaf? Long-haired rocking like The Strokes? Or old-fashioned crooning like Harry Connick Jnr? Biff and Will are particularly proud of a track they've done called *Side By Side*.

"We're trying not to go too pop as he's kind of done that with the great songs he's already covered. We're trying different styles and getting him to

experiment with different textures of his voice. We try and make him understand he is talented and he's not going to be singing covers all his life. *Side By Side* is a great song with an amazing middle eight. It's just beautiful. It's the one we all talk about," says Biff. "That was a great moment. To watch him realise that he can write songs was amazing.

It'll be so different when he stands on stage singing something he's written, because his soul will be on the line. He'll sing it better, there'll be that extra zing to his performance."

In a recent feature in hallowed music magazine *Q*, songwriter Tot Taylor, a man responsible for Mari Wilson's 1982 'hit' *What I Always Wanted*, and who has worked on songs with Michael Jackson and Tina Turner, says of Will's impending album: "When you listen to the songs that are accepted for a Will Young album, you're hearing something stillborn. There's no life because they start predictable and go somewhere predictable." I think it could be a case of Mr Taylor eating his words,

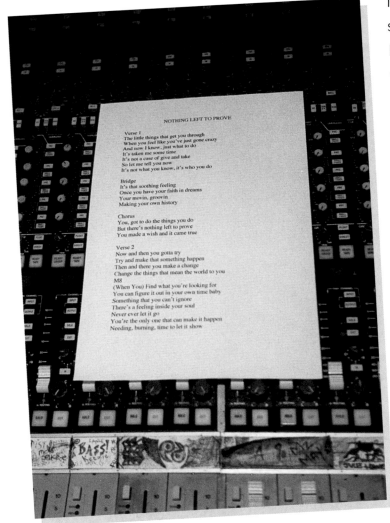

"It'll be so different when he stands
on stage singing something he's written,
because his soul will be on the line.
He'll sing it better, there'll be that extra
zing to his performance."

or choosing another target for his opinions. The song that Will is toying around with is a jazz/blues love song you can imagine a 40s' Trilby-wearing lounge singer whispering in some late night New York bar. It's much more Will. You get the sense that this is the grown-up sort of sound he could only have imagined he would be making. It's anything but predictable.

"It has a real malicious edge to it. It's about a guy who is dumped by this girl, but then she wants him back but he's like, 'I'm sorry, you hurt me, but I'm stronger now and I can only give you so much. Take it or leave it.'"

Will slips into the sound booth to lay down his vocals. When he doesn't nail it first time, he's angry with himself, shouting over the loudspeaker, "Come on Will get it right. Come on!" to inspire him to a better take. His self encouragement seems to do the trick. Biff and Julian have not just been impressed with Will's voice but his attitude to the recording process and his future.

"All artistes must have their own direction, they can't be told where they are going," says Biff. "Will has a definite idea of where he wants to go,

and that perhaps he can't go there straight away and he may have to work his way to that place."

Will puts it like this: "I'm a great list person. I make a list, planning the next two months in advance. My current list says: 1. Finish the album. 2. Release the album. 3. Travel the world."

While he's in Dublin, Will wants to have a go at something typically Celtic – Irish dancing. He has this belief that rather than just passing through cities and countries he should take the time out of his schedule to experience a little culture. "I think it's important when you go to places to try and do something you wouldn't usually do." So the next morning, he books lessons with Olive Hardy, one of Ireland's top Irish dancing coaches. The rehearsal room at Factory Studios, just round the corner from Biff and Julian's place, is all wooden floor and mirrors. Will has even bought his own Hornpike shoes. He's taking this very seriously. There's no warm-up, Will gets straight into learning a straightforward jig, his arms flat by his side.

"I like the fact I don't move my arms. I'm quite a nervous person and I don't know what to do with my

arms when I'm dancing or performing. I did a catwalk show once and I didn't know what to do with them at all. I couldn't walk."

Now I could write a long paragraph about how rubbish Will was at Irish dancing, how he looked like he had two left feet and tripped over, sprawling ungainly into the full-length mirror. But, of course, he was really good at it. From the start. Sickening isn't it?

"I wish I had started dancing from an earlier age. I absolutely love it. I really want to do dance things in the future. I would love to do a musical film. It's all about energy – you completely throw yourself into it. It's all physical, there's no learning lines or learning the notes. I sound quite wanky but I really enjoy it. It's the most impressive performing arts to do. I don't think I could do all the 'be a tree' stuff though. I've always loved dancing, that's why I want to do this film so I can bust some grooves in it!! When I come back to Dublin I'm going to have a lesson every day. I once did a play at school and I played an Irishman with what I thought was a really good accent. A woman came up to me afterwards and went, 'Oh my God, I thought you were amazing, are you Scottish?'. Rather than explaining I was supposed to be Irish I just said, 'Yes I am'."

Despite being tiresomely good at it, let's face it, it still looks a bit silly – legs moving ten to the dozen while the top half is all stiff. I point this out to Will, to which he simply replies grumpily: "Well, I find that very offensive actually. You're not coming to watch again." He turns away, trying to hide a smile.

"I'm quite a nervous person and I don't know what to do with my arms when I'm dancing or performing. I did a catwalk show once and I didn't know what to do with them at all. I couldn't walk."

chapter six

Weather is awful and there is no bloody sunshine – full stop! Oh well, c'est la vie, c u in blackburn.

Time: 18:56

<WILL>

A peaceful Sunday morning in leafy Notting Hill is suddenly shattered by the roar of an engine. A flash of red and black and a new Mini Cooper squeals into view. There's a high-pitched wine of an electric window and out pops Will's grinning face accompanied by some heavy pounding bass. He is test driving a new car for the weekend, and has already tried out what's under the bonnet – "it's got a lot of oomph! It's got a big front end! etc" – by giving the car a run down to Henley-On-Thames to see some friends.

Cars have been an important part of Will's life. He doesn't have a stack of petrol-head magazines next to his toilet, but he's always had an interest in vintage and new models. Will's first car was an old Mini, hence his interest in the new design model he's been zipping around in, and his passion for the automobile stems from his grandad and dad's love of cars.

"I come from a real car family. I think it was because we all wanted to be independent and do our own thing.

"I come from a real car family. I think it was because we all wanted to be independent and do our own thing."

I loved my first Mini, it was in good condition, but picked up a few dents after I had driven it. We used to go to Mini rallies; I remember one at Silverstone that was such a good laugh. They're also a really good car for London – they take corners so well and obviously they don't take up much parking space."

But Will's driving history isn't unblemished. Like most hot-headed young drivers bombing around town in their first car, he fell foul of a dose of late night bad judgement. Something he clearly regrets.

"It was when I was 19. I was in Oxford and went out for the evening, had a few drinks, got drunk and decided to drive home. It was really stupid. I got back outside my house and then decided

I wanted a kebab, which was literally in the next street. I could have walked quicker but instead went down the one-way system the wrong way to get my kebab. A police car drove by, so I quickly went back to my flat. But of course they followed me. I parked, they came up to the window and asked me to get out of the car, but I had parked so badly I couldn't open my door. I then realised I had parked parallel to this sports car and was just bashing my door against it. I eventually got out of the car and was thinking, 'Right, sober, sober, sober' – tripped up in front of them!

"When we got to the police station I was charged and released, but then it got worse. I missed my court hearing. I thought I would wait to receive something through the post. The next day my dad drove me to the police station to get arrested. I had two pairs of handcuffs fitted and put in a holding cell. They took my tie off and took out my shoelaces and then they took my cufflinks away. I was still a bit naïve in those days. In the end I got banned for a year and a half and was fined. It was really good for me. It worked because I would never ever drink and drive again. Looking back it was a good lesson for me

to learn. I was extremely lucky not to have hurt anyone else or myself and drinking and driving is a totally irresponsible thing to do."

Will gets out of one car and into another. This one is a silver Chrysler people carrier – tinted windows, leather seats and 14 cup holders! – to travel in some degree of comfort in up to Blackburn where he is to headline a roadshow for local radio station, Rock FM. It's part and parcel of promotion for a pop singer, and a long list of such dates stretching throughout the summer means Will will be clocking up the miles on the motorways.

"The Swansea one was hysterical. I was in such a funny mood. I did a radio interview down there and they said, 'You're sharing a room with Gareth, what do you think about that?' and I said, 'I'm absolutely disgusted. I can't believe it'. And they believed me because then they said, 'Well Destiny's Child have got two dressing rooms,' and I was like, 'Well now I'm absolutely livid'. I think sometimes people take in everything you say and don't get the joke. It was very muddy at the roadshow and they asked me if Gareth would be wearing his white suit and could he keep

it clean. I said, 'If he does I'll push him in'. I think they finally got the joke in the end.

"Most of the other *Pop Idol* people I'd now count as friends. I don't speak to Rosie at all, but then I saw her at a party the other night and it was lovely to see her and we couldn't stop talking. It's the same with Gareth, he's so busy I just see him when I see him – or text him."

On the way, Will stretches out and reads the Sunday papers. In the *News Of The World* Jay Kay is quoted as saying he would like to record with Will. "Do you think he's taking the piss?" he says modestly, "If he's being serious then that's so nice of him."

"I'd love to pretend that I read a lot but I don't. I've just got back into it after my holiday where I read *Angela's Ashes*. I never get a chance to read the papers. If I had a nine-to-five job I would have time to do that, but I just don't get the time to sit down with papers and have a good read."

Because he's a politics graduate, it's no surprise when he gets stuck into a rather vindictive feature in *The Sunday Times* about Cherie Blair. By and large, the media have so far been, pretty positive about Will's career.

Of course he's had a few negative stories written about him, particularly in the days following the revelations about his sexuality, but Will knows that as supportive as the newspapers have been to him they could easily turn and knock him down.

"I'm sure it's going to come eventually," he says. "They have such an influence over the public. If I say to people, 'Ooh, Richard picks his nose all the time' and keep saying it, then eventually when people talk to you they'll be looking to see if you do, and if they catch you, it will be like 'Oh yeah, you're right, he does'. I know I need to be careful."

As well as respecting the media, Will also respects his ever-growing fan base. Although it's relatively new for him, he's already found that he is under continual scrutiny when he's in public places, and on days when he's feeling under the weather or just in a rush, he tries to remember not to disappoint people who want an autograph or a few words. It may not always be possible, in every situation. But he tries.

"It's just one more thing I have to get my head around. It is really nice. But I have also started to get more panicky.

Sometimes I find it hard to relax in public. It can be scary. I recently went down to Brighton to do some shopping. It was a bit silly really as it was a Saturday and a hot day so the streets were packed. The whole recognising thing had been getting to me. It's weird because you get into this catch 22 situation where you don't want to look to see if people recognise you, but you have to look for it so you know when they are approaching you so you are prepared for it. Anyway, I walked out of the car park on to the main street and a woman spotted me and came over. I'd made a decision not to sign autographs and to pretend to be somebody else. Silly really. I put on this East End accent and went, 'No, sorry luv, I'm not Will'. There were people watching on the other side of the street and I knew that if I signed one I would be there all afternoon. It was my day off, and I was in a rush as I only had a couple of hours to get loads of presents and things. A few days later a letter turned up at the management company from a lady. I was really pleased actually as I felt so guilty and it gave me a chance to write back and make amends. People will probably think I'm being stupid and that I should be expected to always take time out to speak to anybody who comes up to me, but they don't see what goes on. You finish work for the day and then you have people approaching you in the car, in the street, in the restaurant, on the way home."

Referencing back to the incident with the fan in the Kensington café, Will admits it's the lack of manners from some people that really get him annoyed.

"You could ask my teachers at school and they'll tell you that good manners have always been a thing of mine. I think some people come across as rude or arrogant as they are nervous when they meet you."

He always has time for polite fans, but when he gets grabbed or has pieces of paper shoved in his face the chances of a well-written love ode or flourishing friendship are very remote.

"I've learnt a lesson about that, and I've written it down in my journal and now I'm fine with it. You can't judge people by your own standards otherwise you are always going to be wound up. I probably have very high standards on manners, or I'm a perceptive person and would judge what is right and wrong, but you can't judge people by what my standards are. You could ask my teachers at school and they'll tell you that good manners have always been a thing of mine. I think some people come across as rude or arrogant as they are nervous when they meet you. I guess that's why you shouldn't judge people by the first meeting either."

Ewood Park, the home of Blackburn Rovers, Premiership football club. But instead of Damien Duff dribbling in the penalty area it's 20,000 teenage girls. They've been soaking up the sun all afternoon and warming up their lungs by screaming at Mis-Teeq, Daniel Beddingfield, 3SL and, strangely,

"Of course I know I'm also doing an unusual job, but it's just that. I think that's what keeps me level headed because I treat it like a business although it is also my passion."

Chesney Hawkes. But the majority are here to see Will. Lower down on the bill is Will's ex-*Pop Idol* compatriot Darius, but unfortunately by the time we arrive, he's already left the stadium. "I don't see him that much," says Will. "I think he's very busy. He's doing his own thing. He's quite an enigma as a person."

Backstage, in one of the small dressing rooms, Will has just been informed that he's meeting a couple of competition winners. It's the first he knew about it. An email sent to him with all the details didn't arrive, lost to one of the many glitches on the information superhighway, and it's got him a little annoyed. But it's not because he doesn't want to meet them, pose for a picture and sign some autographs, it's because he likes things neatly planned in front of

him. He likes to wake up in the morning and think, 'Right I have this, this and this to do today'. He would have liked to have known what the competition was, how they won it and prepared something special for them.

"I'm not a control freak, I just like to know things in advance. I like to know where I'm going and what I'm doing. I enjoy meeting competition winners like today. I'm conscious of keeping part of me private. I was once asked to record my voice on to a phone as a promotion and I felt I was giving away too much of me. It's like, 'Here, take a finger'. Of course I know I'm also doing an unusual job, but it's just that. I think that's what keeps me level headed because I treat it like a business although it is also my passion. It keeps my feet on the ground. In the future I might look back and think, 'Hmm, I shouldn't have done that', but I don't think I will. I don't feel like I'm being manipulated. I know there are other people who don't have it as easy as me. I have friends who are doing the same thing as me and have different management, and they're arseholes as far as I can see. I'm with nice people who are very good at what they do – so we all work together."

The side of the stage is like a rugby scrum. People with their chests puffed with self importance jostle for a view of Will singing *Evergreen* and *Light My Fire*. In the sea of bodies in front of him banners are waved, teddies are thrown and even one girl, proudly sporting a T-shirt with Gareth's face on it, is singing along with gusto. Will is adopting his usual singing stance – microphone in one hand, the other, bent at the elbow, stuck out to the side.

"During *Pop Idol* everyone used to call me Teapot Man because I look like I'm doing a teapot impression," he says after making a mad dash off stage and straight into the car. "You always knew when I was into my performance because one hand would be on my side the other stuck out like the spout of a teapot. My mum said, 'Joe Cocker used to do that', and when I saw him at the Jubilee I saw that he does do a similar thing. I must have unconsciously logged that away in my head at some point."

If there was any question that Will had 'made it' the next few minutes lay any lingering doubts to rest. With a roar of motorbike engines and a burst of flashing red and blue lights he's given a police escort out of Blackburn. A service only reserved for royalty. Until now.

chapter seven

How is concrete London? Lovely 2 b at home with
doggies. Am still thinking of my five favourite songs.
c u later 4 a pint. A demain...

Time: 12:08

<WIl l >

We have a lot to thank our Italian cousins for – cracking tomato based food, delicate red wines, pretty good footballers, aqueducts – and Italy is also the birth place of that strange cultural art, the opera. Ever since the 14th Century blind composer Francesco Landini started playing about with the *caccia* (a musical piece about hunting), they've been churning out long pieces of music that can only be sung by fat fellas. Among the most well known is *La Traviata*, a heartbreaking tale of a courtesan who falls in love, gets insulted by her beloved's father and tragically dies. Over the years it has captivated even the most uneducated of opera goers – most notably Julia Roberts' prostitute with a heart of gold who blubbed her way through the final act in *Pretty Woman*. Will is determined to broaden his cultural horizons, and so with that in mind has chosen to see a production of Guiseppe Verdi's greatest work at the Royal Albert Hall as his first taste of opera.

"I've always wanted to see one, but have never got round to it," he says. "I like to think I've listened to a wide range of music, but for some reason have never really got into opera. I've heard it's beautiful though."

Accompanying Will to his box is his friend Katie Russel, herself a trained singer, who he lived with at Exeter University and who he's remained friends with since moving to London. The pair were members of Footlights, the drama society, and worked together on a number of projects including Oklahoma – which Katie produced and in which Will played the leading role of Curly.

"I remember one night the curtains went up, the music started and the spotlight lit up an empty stage – there was no Will," says Katie. "We were in such a panic and frantically trying to find him. In the end we found him backstage just pottering around, not aware of the time. I could have killed him."

Katie is just one of a whole group of university friends that Will still sees now.

"I got to know a whole lot of people through Footlights who I'm still friends with – Katie, Andy, Tom, Adam, Steph, Sarah and Rachel – we really bonded. Actually, thinking about it, we probably weren't very nice to anyone else. It's funny because we formed such a strong friendship, but at the time I didn't think I did. It became a running joke that I would never go to the Footlights socials

Account No. 20614728

ROYAL ALBERT HALL

Door 6
Grand Tier
Box 25
Seat 001

Ellen Kent and Opera International present
LA TRAVIATA

Thursday, 27 June 2002
at 7:15 PM
Doors open at 6:30 PM

£ 49.00
FULL
PHN CRED

2002   LATRO1   Q

and hang out with these people. They probably thought I was snotty. There was a bit of a public school thing there which did my head in. I hate categories, I hate thinking people put you in categories like, 'Right, you're private school so you are going to be like this' or, 'You're gay so you're going to be like this'. I think you should just do and be whatever you want to. It's easier, though, to hang on to an identity allocated to you rather than find your own."

Will studied politics at uni – he eventually got a 2:2 – and he first became interested in the subject at school where he took A levels in politics, history and English. He even went so far as to join a local demonstration.

"I was 18 and a member of the eco society and was making this documentary about the demonstrations to try and stop the Newbury Bypass being built. I said I was doing work experience for a few days but went along and filmed all

"I grew up listening to my mother's music. She's great, she's much hipper than I am. She talks about bands I've never heard of. I went home recently and she had a long list of music she wanted to get and I didn't recognise half the names."

these people in trees and charging cranes. But I got caught on the local news. The house master walked in, and the TV was on and the rest of the dorm tried to distract him from it, because all you could see was me charging down with my camera and falling over as all these protestors started burning this crane."

However, his interest in politics waned during university, but he still looks up to some political figures – he cites Tony Benn as one. "To be honest, I've never really been that interested in current affairs. I would love to go on something like *Question Time*, but I don't know enough about it and would just look like an idiot. I think it's something I'll get into more when I'm older."

Disillusioned with sitting through politics lessons, Will concentrated on his performing and singing. However, he found that university wasn't conducive to improving his voice and he was forced to go down a different avenue to refine his singing techniques.

"I was quite repressed with my singing. Of course I did the musicals but that was it really. So when we had been out, on the way home from the clubs we used to cut through this car park, which had great acoustics and would just start singing. Sometimes for two or three hours at a time. It was mad. I remember one time a woman leaned out of her upstairs window and told us to shut up as she had a young boy trying to get to sleep, so we all

crowded round under window and sang Gershwin as a sort of lullaby to get him to sleep. She stuck her head out again and told us to push off as it clearly wasn't working. I think we slightly missed the point!"

Unlike most teenagers with their musical tastes shaped by their peers – "Hey, if he's into Level 42 I should be!" – Will's love of music really stems from his parents, particularly his mum.

"I grew up listening to my mother's music. She's great, she's much hipper than I am. She talks about bands I've never heard of. I went home recently and she had a long list of music she wanted to get and I didn't recognise half the names – it was stuff like Zero 7. God knows. So she's always been into music. When I was growing up I was into Paul Simon, Tracy Chapman, Sade, Otis Redding, Aretha Franklin, The Eurythmics and always The Beatles. Not so much The Rolling Stones.

"I've always liked soul music really, particularly female vocalists, but I've recently discovered Stevie Wonder and am really getting into him now. To be honest I haven't really had the chance to buy lots of CDs. I'm going to get a

load of big bags and go down to second-hand record shops and just binge on CDs. At the moment I'm listening to Lauryn Hill and Inda Irie, Angie Stone, Jil Scott. I like jazz soul singers. It really depends what mood I'm in. The only thing I've never been into is heavy rock. I just don't get it.

Although what's on his Walkman changes from day to day, depending on his mood, the five songs he wants played at his funeral remain constant:

1. Joan Armatrading *Love And Affection*
2. Paul Simon *Hearts And Bones*
3. Aretha Franklin *Angel*
4. The Beatles *Day In The Life*
5. Tracy Chapman *Fast Car*

Most people who attend the opera make a bit of an effort with their attire. Throughout the auditorium there're ladies in flowing gowns and men in suits. Will doesn't really do smart. He just doesn't feel comfortable in it. Although he's wearing a brown and black striped blazer, he's also wearing a scruffy looking pair of cords, trainers and an old T-shirt.

"My look hasn't drastically changed since the show, the stuff I wear now is the same as I wore a few years ago, it's just that I get more access to clothes now. Like I'll go, 'Oh I really want a jumper like that' and I'll be able to get one. I've always been interested in fashion – again, my mum has always been very stylish and good at putting things together. I think it rubbed off on me. At university I used to spend loads of money on clothes. I'd get my student loan and go down to the shopping streets in Exeter and spend. I liked the second-hand and surf shops. There's a great shop called The Real McCoy which sells second-hand vintage clothes and has got a great café as well. I liked the places where everything on one rail would be a pound."

After winning the show, Will didn't sit down with a team of stylists and come up with what defines the 'Will look'. There was no head scratching, hastily drawn sketches and ideas of dressing him in boiler suits and flower covered hats which would "So make an impact darrrhhhling!". Pretty much how you see Will today is what he would have looked like nipping in and out of the shops on Exeter High Street.

"The only thing that has slightly changed is my opinion of suits. When I started the show I said I would not be

"My look hasn't drastically changed since the show, the stuff I wear now is the same as I wore a few years ago, it's just that I get more access to clothes now. Like I'll go, 'Oh I really want a jumper like that' and I'll be able to get one."

seen dead in a suit. I hate suits, I hate them. But then I started to get given them and try them out and actually I have started to wear them. But I try and wear them with trainers or with a T-shirt. I'd never wear the suit with a shirt and tie combo, it's a bit too much like a bank manager. Armani has always been a favourite of mine. I could never really afford his stuff though. I would have trips to London and walk past the shops and just look through the window. I think my look is hippy scruff.

After the opera has finished Will feels really cultured – he loved the music, enjoyed the Karaoke style words that flashed above the actors' heads and yet, despite all the grandiose imagery and

tear inducing sentimental overtones, it was the smallest detail that intrigued him. He spent the whole opera considering the career of one of the minor characters. Halfway through an elderly gentleman, dressed in a bright red coat, playing the role of a servant – wandering around on stage handing out flutes of champagne to the guests at the make-believe party.

"I wonder if that's what he does for a living? He's a jobbing actor who goes down the pub and says to his mates, 'Yeah, I've got a gig tomorrow at the Albert Hall. Yeah, it's a small role.' Has he trained all his life for that type of part or did he really want to play the bigger main roles?"

chapter eight

Ola! Stuck in Glastonbury traffic. Enjoyed opera
the other night, we r posh rn't we?!

Time: 11:58

<WILL>

The first thing you notice about Warsaw is not the juxtaposition of modern and Stalinesque architecture, nor the fact that it's a much more beautiful city than your preconceptions would have had you believe. No, it's the fact that nearly every male you encounter has decided to cultivate an enormous moustache. It's as if, at the first whiff of puberty, Poland's teenage boys are told in no uncertain terms to nurture and prune an elaborate lip brush. But none are more impressive than that of our taxi driver – whose moustache is like a trailing ivy in a hanging basket, drooping over his mouth and flying up with every exhale as he guides us through the city centre. Thankfully, facial topiary is not high up on Will's list of priorities.

"I sometimes have a bit more stubble, like today, and I like to look a bit more manly now and again, but moustaches are maybe not the way forward. I remember when I was young and got that first bit of fluff and thought I was so grown up and that it was proper facial hair. You'd shave but there really wasn't anything there. You almost wanted to cut yourself shaving so you could go in to school and go, 'Oh this? It's just a knick. Yeah, I cut myself shaving'. I started growing proper hair when I was 15, and had a bit of a hairy lip. I think I would go for a full-on beard rather than bits over the face. I think it would happen more out of laziness because I hate shaving."

This is Will's first time in Poland and his first international press engagement. He's here to perform at the final of this country's *Pop Idol* – simplified to just *Idol* for the Polish TV audience – and is aware that the evening is going to throw up a mixture of memories, both good and bad.

"I remember the week before the final show there were three of us, I was so nervous. But on the final I was completely calm. Although if you watch me perform the three songs you can see how happy I am when I'm singing *Light My Fire* as I knew that it was all over and I could relax. But I can't believe I'm back doing a final again. It's so weird."

Today is probably the most chilled I've seen Will. He spent the day before at the Glastonbury Festival with his sister Emma watching Beverly Knight and Ian Brown – "I'm definitely going next year, I'm blocking the whole weekend out in the diary now." He even found time to buy some bangles for friends and some joss-sticks – their sandalwood aroma fills the dressing room.

The studio set bears an uncanny resemblance to the one that became so familiar to Will and the rest of the nation. There's the logo, the dreaded panel sofa and the theme music which keeps pounding out of the many speakers dotted around the studio. It's a little unnerving. *Idol* has been just as big a success here in Poland as in the UK, regularly drawing six million viewers, which, from a populace of 38.7 million, is not a bad ratio.

Will sings *Light My Fire* for the dress rehearsal. It doesn't go well. There're problems where the sound is coming from, for Will to hear where he is in the song, and the technicians can't get the reverb right. The floor manager (moustachioed obviously) turns to Will and states, "I'm only doing my job," to which Will quite rightly retorts, "Yes, well I'm only doing my job." It's not going swimmingly.

"I was nervous down there," he confides later. "There were all the Polish contestants watching and all I could think was that they were probably saying, 'Hmm, he's not very good is he? How did he win the UK show?' I think, when I get nervous, I can come across as arrogant sometimes."

After a bowl of traditional Polish fare, *Borscht* – "You've got to try these things haven't you?" – Will is ready for the show. Unlike the UK finale, there are three contenders for the *Idol* crown. A petite blonde girl, sort of a cross between Hannah from S Club and Samantha Janus, called Alicja Janosz. A hippy-looking girl – think Natalie Imbruglia crossed with Holly Valance – Ewelina Flinta, and a long-haired Michael Bolton wannabe Szymon Wydra. Instead of cheeky Geordies keeping proceedings running along

smoothly, there's a Zoe Ball-alike in a silver dress and a moody looking teenage boy in a white suit.

Before going on Will makes sure he phones his mum. One thing you notice about Will is that he's never far from his phone. It bleeps every five minutes. And when it stays silent for a short while, you can catch him picking it up and asking the phone's display why he hasn't got any messages. His relationship with his phone and how often it is in his hands is also an indication of how he's feeling. If his thumbs – honestly, you've never seen a pair of thumbs move so fast – are constantly hammering away at the buttons it's usually because there's something wrong.

"You'll know if I've had a bad day or something bad has happened because I'll be on my phone a lot, I'll be texting my friends or family with just a short little, 'bad day help'."

It's clear from spending time with Will that he's very close to his family and will always make time for visits and phone calls, even if it's just for a few minutes – he stayed with his parents on the way back from Glastonbury before making his way to Heathrow.

"When we were on the show my mum gave all of the contestants pocket

His relationship with his phone and how often it is in his hands is also an indication of how he's feeling. If his thumbs – honestly, you've never seen a pair of thumbs move so fast – are constantly hammering away at the buttons it's usually because there's something wrong.

He's very protective of his mum Annabel and dad Robin. "They didn't ask for this attention, and I don't want them not to be able to go about their day without getting pestered. I love them too much to do that to them."

animals. Our family has this terrible habit of buying toys for our cousins and nephews and ending up keeping them for ourselves. I remember in Glasgow, when we were on tour, we all brought our pocket animals on stage. I was singing *My Way*, and I had my little animal next to the microphone and was singing to it."

And yet he's very protective of his mum Annabel and dad Robin. Although he'll mention them in passing and lots of his stories will begin with them, he carefully avoids any direct questions about them, or asks them not to be written in the book. "They didn't ask for this attention, and I don't want them not to be able to go about their day without getting pestered. I love them too much to do that to them."

It was at Glastonbury that Will had another epiphany about dealing with attention from people. "I've got my head around it a bit more now. You've got to remember that for them it's just five seconds, and that's the only time they are going to have with you. You have to bear that in mind. Glastonbury was such an open event, there was nowhere to hide, and I'm really pleased with the way it went. I managed to keep a low profile by keeping my head down and walking quick. But I was really relaxed with people. I think this was a turning point for me and I'm obviously getting used to it. You have to be polite. I think I learned how to do that from my university days. It's like where you meet loads of people at the start of term and by the end of the year you have your

close friends and the people you just know. I learned how to walk into the bar and say hello to the people I met at the beginning of term too, but spent most of my time with my close friends."

The earlier problems are a distant memory as Will cracks out a tight version of *Light My Fire*, despite the disturbing presence of what looks like early 90s' rave video graphics swirling on the screens behind him. He then has a short interview with the bizarre looking presenters who ask him what he thought of the judges. It's almost like an early episode of *Star Trek*, and that we've fallen through some strange space time continuum and ended up in a parallel version of Earth, except that instead of Simon Cowell there's a blond, dreadlocked music critic dolling out patronising advice to the three finalists. Will has taken an immediate dislike to him, and unlike the UK show when Will had to bite his tongue when confronted by the judges, Will tells him in no uncertain terms exactly what he thought of his comments to the contestants.

"I was pleased I had a go at him," says Will afterwards. "I thought he was so mean. I quite liked going on that stage in the end. I felt like a rebellious pupil."

chapter nine

Did you know that the Latin for Golden Eagle is 'Aquila Chysaetis'? ...now obviously not really exciting but not bad info for a Monday morning!!

Time: 10:04

<WILL>

It's no surprise that wannabe London cab drivers can take up to three years learning the 'knowledge' – the in-depth understanding of the highways and byways of our capital. There are so many tiny lanes and backstreets almost wanting to be kept a secret, that can trip up even the most well-informed taxi driver. In one of these tiny mews, just off Kensington High Street, is The Grenadier pub. It has real olde-worlde charm. Beams and horsebrasses. There's barely room inside to swing a cat – in fact the said feline would have its head embedded in the wall before half a revolution. Thankfully, it's a warm night and the pub's patrons have spilled on to the cobbled street. Among them are Will, his non-identical twin Rupert and friends Pilky, Rose, Jim and Andy. The vodka and oranges are slipping down nicely. The plates of sausage and chips are being ravenously consumed to soak up the alcohol. This is Will at his most casual. He laughs. A lot. There's no massive ego. There's no petulant pop star arrogance. Even when

"I think my relationship with my friends has become closer since doing the show. Definitely."

a group of overweight bankers in ill-fitting shirts and trousers start making snide remarks, Will lets it ride over him, ignores their comments and returns to the comfort of being surrounded by friends.

"I think my relationship with my friends has become closer since doing the show. Definitely. When I was doing *Pop Idol*, that was all the conversation

would be about. But now, as things get less new and we all get used to it, we just talk about our jobs, and I've become more conscious not to talk about it. I think I see more of my friends now than I used to before. You just need your friends big time."

But does he think their attitude has changed towards him? Do they treat him like a big time Charlie, or the same old Will with his slightly crooked chin?

"I don't think so. I think they thought I was always going to sing (I hope they thought that?!). It's like my feelings towards them. I have faith in their abilities to achieve what they want in life. The show was like one big party, we had a party and piss-up after every one.

"I think I see more of my friends now than I used to before. You just need your friends big time."

And there was never such a legitimate excuse for a piss-up. We hark back to it sometimes and we are like, 'What was it like every week?'. I would always pop out for a quick beer every Friday and it would be, 'Well, I might see you on Sunday or I'll see you Saturday night'. It was odd. But we all slipped into the routine and when it was over, we all had a big gap in our Saturday nights, we felt like, 'No more piss-ups, no more excuses'."

He also values their comments and advice on the songs he's been recording and is keen for them to like what's come out of the Dublin sessions. "They're all really excited. I always play them songs, especially to Pilky and Milsy. Friends' approval means a lot to me. I will only talk about the job to a certain amount of people. There's a whole secrecy thing which is an odd conversation to have with them at first. Like one friend said to me, 'I hope you know that you can tell me things and I'm not going to tell people,' it was nice that we cleared it up and moved on. You need to have that conversation with them because this is a funny business that I'm in."

If there's a party going on, Will

"We used to go to this pub opposite a bakery and we used to call an all-day session a Princess Leia and pop over the road to get a couple of Danish pastries to stick to the sides of our heads."

might not be the life and soul of it but it certainly wouldn't be short of laughter – if not always in response to his wisecracks.

"I can be quite daft sometimes. I've always been jokey with friends and always cracking bad gags. I wouldn't say I was the type of person who turns up and suddenly, 'Hey, the whole night is swinging', but hopefully I don't turn up and everyone goes, 'Oh god…it's him'. My friends have been so good to me, I used up a lot of credits in the bank when I was feeling down and they cheered me up, so I try and look to help them out as much as possible. Although a family trait is that we Youngs don't listen. I just switch off, but I do try and listen when it's important and I do my best to give good advice. I'm quite intuitive, I guess I have a feeling when

people are unhappy. I tend to work people out quite quickly. It's a good thing to have, I get that from my dad."

As the drinks slide down, the sausages get eaten and Will's legendary drinking stories crawl out of the woodwork. Although these days he's careful about quaffing too much beer – he's conscious about avoiding the deadly booze and hangover if he has to work the next day – Will did plenty of drinking in his uni days.

"We used to go to this pub opposite a bakery and we used to call an all-day session a Princess Leia and pop over the road to get a couple of Danish pastries to stick to the sides of our heads. I had been out on one of these and I tried to walk home late at night but I fell flat on my face and cut my head. It was quite warm so I took off my shirt and started to head for home, but the blood was pouring out of my wound. I had blood all over me. It was like I'd walked straight off a horror film set. The next day a friend said to me, 'Oh yeah, I drove past you when you were walking home last night, you didn't look very well'. And I was like, 'Well you could have bloody helped me'."

Will's brother Rupert, has recently been getting attention from people, they know him after he was featured on *Pop Idol*. Of course it could be worse – imagine what it would be like if he looked exactly the same as Will!! But Will is keen to keep Rupert, like his parents, out of the unwanted limelight.

There were huge benefits in growing up as one half of a twin as there was always another person the same age to hang around with.

"It was brilliant, because you have an ally in everything you do. We both have a fierce protectiveness of each other. When we went through boarding school it was great to have someone else there. We were in the same houses and I always had someone to play with. I can't imagine what it must be like to be an only child."

And of course there were fights: "We used to have huge bust-ups. The worst

There were huge benefits in growing up as one half of a twin as there was always another person the same age to hang around with. "It was brilliant, because you have an ally in everything you do. We both have a fierce protectiveness of each other."

was when he shot me with an air rifle. I was about 16, it was the summer holiday and I would practise basketball on the tennis court – typical me really, I always focus on one thing, and do it until I get good at it. I wanted to be captain of the basketball team so I was practising shooting hoops all summer – I heard a window open. I looked round and saw the nozzle of the air rifle peek out of the window. And he shot me in the leg, shouted 'Don't wake me up again' and slammed the window. After that it kicked off big time."

The bullet wound and the slight limp, didn't stop Will playing basketball or tennis at school. But no amount of encouragement could get him in the firing line on the cricket square at Horris Hill school.

"I was useless at cricket, I was scared of being hit by the ball – it's just so small and hard. Cricket is a horrible game. Instead I was the groundsman. We would play twice a week and, with my friend Benjamin, my job was to take the covers off the swimming pool, make the cocoa and take it out to the players on this trolley. It was like something out of Billy Bunter. We'd jump on the trolley and ride it down the hill, crash, and the cocoa and buns would go everywhere. We'd then take it out to the cricketers, set up in the pavilion, eat all the nice cakes and leave the ones that had fallen off the trolley for everyone else. The one time I did actually go into bat, I just told the bowler, 'Right, if you bowl that thing fast at me I'm going to break your neck'. But then I realised that if I hit my own wicket I would be out. So before anyone could bowl at me I'd push the bat back and go, 'Oh my God, I don't believe it. I'm out! How on earth did that happen?'."

Not that Will's parents were spared attending sports galas to watch their sons in action.

"We would have these diving competitions and all the parents would always insist on coming. At first I could never work out why. The first students, the good ones at diving, would do a dive, and it would be perfect, very little splash. But as they worked their way down the line the dives would just get worse and worse till it was the boy at the end doing a belly flop. He'd flop into the water with this enormous splash and all you could hear was the mums and dads roaring with laughter."

chapter ten

I'm thinking McDonalds – perhaps not the healthiest option!

Time: 17.43

<WILL>

Will and I have a similar attitude to ordering a takeaway from McDonalds. If you opt for a quarter pound and cheese with fries (large, obviously), it's never going to satisfy you. It's much better to add a few extras into your bag, just to finish the job. Better to be safe than sorry. There would be nothing worse than swallowing the last mouthful and still have a hollow sensation in the stomach. Tonight Will's added two more cheeseburgers. And a banana milkshake.

It's a horrible Thursday evening. The rain thunders on to the window pane despite it being early July. However, inside Will's top floor flat it's a chilled atmosphere. There's a little known American female artiste Janis Ian on the stereo. The sagging sofas are groaning under the weight of far too much consumed burgers and the dreary weather outside is soon forgotten. It's incredibly clean in Will's flat. There's no running your finger along the mantlepiece and finding it covered in fluff.

"Whenever I had a spare moment or was in the flat on my own, I would clean. I think I needed that sense of organising and it was relaxing. I had to get a cleaner in the end because it stopped me constantly tidying. I'm the sort of person who can't sit down unless everything is just so around me."

"When I'm here on my own I'm a terrible faffer. I clean a lot. After the show, whenever I had a spare moment or was in the flat on my own, I would clean. I think I needed that sense of organising and it was relaxing. I had to get a cleaner in the end because it stopped me constantly tidying. I'm the sort of person who can't sit down unless everything is just so around me."

Having spent a fair bit of time in Will's company when he's been holding interviews with the media, he's careful about what he gives away about certain parts of his private life. When probed by interviewers he tends to laugh it off or make a subtle joke diverting attention away from what they are really trying to get out of him. It's a technique that some celebrities take years to master – only after countless kiss and tell exposées in the Sunday papers do they twig that they really don't have to give explicit details about all their nocturnal activities in every interview. Relaxing on the sofa, alternating between sipping his milkshake and glass of wine – perhaps not to everyone's taste – tonight his guard is down.

OK, Will, let's talk about relationships.

"There's not a lot to say."

Would you just go out and have a one night stand?

"I was speaking to a friend about this the other day. I was round his house and this girl came into the room and blatantly wanted to be with him. We went out to the car to say goodbye, and I said, 'My God, she really fancies you' and I was like, 'Get in there!', and he was like, 'Why bother?' and we both decided sometimes there's no point."

Would you really like to have a relationship now?

"I'm quite chilled out about it. I don't really think about it that much, I'm quite an independent person anyway."

Do you believe in love?

"Oh yes, massively."

You said you were romantic. In what ways?

"Not in a 'Let's go out for candlelit dinners', but I've always been quite mushy – more romantic in a sentimental way. If you were to describe it as a movie, I'm more *Remains Of The Day* than *French Kiss*.

By the time we finish talking it's the early hours and Will is stretched out on the sofa. He'll be getting only a few hours' sleep, as there's an interview to do at 8am the next morning.

chapter eleven

Heard some great chat up lines the other day 'I do like your clothes but they'd look better crumpled on the bedroom floor' – these are generic obviously!

Time: 13:02

<WILL>

Grey and overcast clouds hang over London's Hyde Park. Not even snake-hips Enrique, wiggling his leather-trouser-clad bottom can nudge the sun out of hiding. It's the sort of day where you take your jacket off, put your jacket on, and then take it off again. But the 60,000 crowd are undeterred and still cheer enthusiastically every time Dr Fox, in a rather dapper pin-striped suit, sprints on to the stage to announce the next act. It's Capital Radio's Party In The Park, its annual shindig in aid of the Prince's Trust. In this year's line-up are Natalie Imbruglia, Ashanti, the 'Groover from Vancouver' Bryan Adams, Shakira, Westlife, Atomic Kitten and, of course, Queen. Also on the bill are Will and Gareth. They're sharing a dressing room again. It's the first time I've seen the two of them together and they greet each other with a hug before diving into a quick

Also on the bill are Will and Gareth. It's the first time I've seen the two of them together and they greet each other with a hug before diving into a quick catch-up. Although certain sections of the media might like to conspire conflicts between the two, it's evident that the reports are ill founded. They're quite clearly friends.

catch-up. Although certain sections of the media might like to conspire conflicts between the two, it's evident that the reports are ill founded. They're quite clearly friends.

This event is about 10 times the size of the roadshow in Blackburn with more acts, more people, more press and more food – a 200-metre hospitality marquee stretches along one side of the backstage area.

Will pretty much stays in his dressing room – a small Portakabin opposite the one assigned for A1 and two doors along from Ashanti – with fans attempting to peer through the window and the slats in the Venetian blind. We're discussing Will's future. Any wizened old crone peering into a crystal ball would struggle to predict with total certainty where he's headed. The fickleness of the British record-buying public could mean that come the end of 2002 Mr Young is a distant memory. Maybe it's the mood Will's in today, he's just being pragmatic, or perhaps he's had an epiphany about this job he's doing, but he seems more negative than usual about the business he's in.

"I absolutely adore the music, and I have so much confidence in my talent, but I wonder sometimes if I can handle it. Maybe the music will keep me going. I'm not unhappy, I have nothing to be unhappy about. But I find conflicts very difficult and I have had so many of them. All very amicable really, and about small things, but I've realised that I don't like them, and I've become this person who keeps having them. It's so draining because you have to stand your ground. It takes up quite a lot in me, to speak up. I'm bad at saying 'no' but I think that's part of growing up and part of any job.

"All jobs have their ups and downs, and if I'm honest I'm finding today hard. I'm sure I'm no different to anyone else. I'm 23, and by the time I'm 30 if I was still singing, I would like to be an established artist. I don't think seven years is a presumptuous time. Two years is, but seven years is fair enough. I would like to think that by then there would be no more doubts about whether

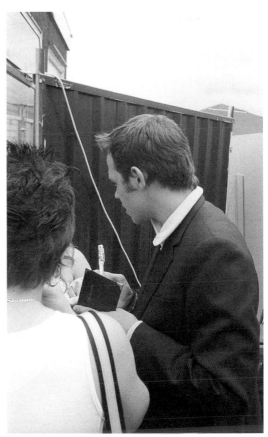

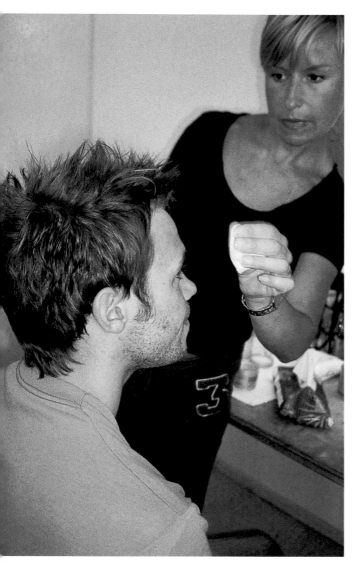

I can last. If Robbie Williams finished today it would be like 'Yes he did it and was established'. The same for Kylie. I'd like that to be me when I'm 30. It would be fantastic to be able to go, 'Right, now I'm going to be a hippy and live in Tanzania'."

When Will does get into these down moods it's the fans who pick him up and keep him going. The reception he gets when performing his three hits, *Ain't No Sunshine*, *Evergreen* and *Light My Fire* keeps him going, even through the hour and a half of TV interviews, radio interviews, print interviews and photographs he immediately does after coming off stage.

"I'm loving the fans at the moment, they send the best letters. They are so cool, particularly the older women. There was one from a 63-year-old who was going to knock the people who were having a go at me with her umbrella.

"I absolutely adore the music, and I have so much confidence in my talent, but I wonder sometimes if I can handle it. Maybe the music will keep me going."

They always say the same sort of things – keep on smiling, stay the way you are, don't ever change – it's always that. I try to reply to as many as I can."

Having not known Will before *Pop Idol* and before his solo career, I'm intrigued to find out if he thinks he's changed at all.

"No, I don't think so. I run the risk of becoming a bit bitchier. That could be an industry thing. It's not usually about people, it's just little asides about things. I have to stop and go to myself, 'Oh don't go down that route'. It can only be damaging."

Over the past couple of weeks, Will has been ploughing on with the album and the amount of songs he's completed is growing ever bigger. It looks like he'll have enough material to fill two albums. What he's most pleased about is the variety of music he's laying down. And the intriguing collaborations that have come his way.

"I go through stages of being really nervous and thinking 'Oh God is this album any good, are people going to like it?' but I think this comes with the job, self doubt happens in any profession and you just have to ride through it and trust in what you are doing. Part of it is that I find it difficult to describe what kind of sound I'm putting out there but on reflection I think that is a good thing. The tunes all denote a very melancholic sound and it has been fun to really try and explore the tones in my voice and to try and bring those out in the studio.

Something like the Burt Bacharach song is a very smooth, mellow tune and is a great example of a track that isn't perhaps as raw as some of the songs I sing. *You and I*, for example, is a slightly more rousing song and I go to town on it a bit more at the end. I've realised that on an album, every song has to have it's own place and to have variety is great. There is a big difference between something like *Evergreen* (the first track on the album) and something like *Fineline* which is simply me and 30 strings and is alot darker."

Whatever happens, Will doesn't contain his excitement about performing his new material. "Doing covers has been great, and even though I have come under pressure for doing them, I think they have more than earned their place on the album and they carry a bit of *Pop Idol* history with them which I think is great. Everyone likes a bit of nostalgia!"

If the music doesn't work, Will has one eye on a film career. The idea first surfaced in his brain during his university days. And the more he thinks about it, the more appealing the thought is.

"I've been getting really arty farty and thinking up all these ideas and writing them down. I started a film script when I was supposed to be revising for my exams. I'm waiting till I get my own house and then will start work on it properly with my friend Adam Jones who's an actor. I think it could work, it would be so cool for me to do. I've got a few people in mind, one being Jane Horrocks. I think she's a great actress. I'm really nervous about it, it might have to be one of those things that I don't think about I just take on and do."

If Will does go down the acting route, you might see him treading in his hero's footsteps – Anthony Hopkins – although whether that will mean eating his enemy's liver with some fava beans and washed down with a nice Chianti remains to be seen.

"I am a big fan of him. He's amazing at what he does, but tends to keep himself to himself and leads what seems to be a very normal life. If I can manage to keep my feet this firmly on the ground and be that established, I'd be more than happy. Here I am six months into being a solo artist and about to launch my first album. I've really enjoyed making it, particularly the original material. The proof of the pudding will be in the eating."

Will and I meet for one brief and final time. He plays me the near as damn it completed album. It's exhilarating to hear that the rough and ready track demos I heard on the stereo of a silver people carrier (14 cup holders!) on the way to Blackburn, on his Discman sitting on the floor of a bleak Warsaw dressing room or booming out of the sound booth of a studio in Dublin have now been turned into slick, fully fleshed-out songs. It's a rich and eclectic sounding album, which won't disappoint the already addicted Will Young fans but will surely enchant a whole legion of new ones. It may even find itself on my stereo (although I'm sure Will won't mind me skipping over *Evergreen* and *Light My Fire* – I think I've heard them quite enough times already!).

Since starting this book all my friends have been keen to know exactly what Will's like. Well, he's not the grinning buffoon I originally had him down as... he is, well, how can I put it? A thoroughly "nice bloke".

"They always say the same sort of things – keep on smiling, stay the way you are, don't ever change – it's always that. I try to reply to as many as I can."